# Process Modeling Style

# Process Modeling Style

By John Long
OMG Certified Expert in BPM (OCEB)

ELSEVIER

AMSTERDAM • BOSTON • HEIDELBERG • LONDON
NEW YORK • OXFORD • PARIS • SAN DIEGO
SAN FRANCISCO • SINGAPORE • SYDNEY • TOKYO

Morgan Kaufmann is an imprint of Elsevier

Morgan Kaufmann is an imprint of Elsevier
225 Wyman Street, Waltham, MA, 02451, USA

**Notices**
Knowledge and best practice in this field are constantly changing. As new research and experience broaden our understanding, changes in research methods or professional practices, may become necessary.

Practitioners and researchers must always rely on their own experience and knowledge in evaluating and using any information or methods described herein. In using such information or methods they should be mindful of their own safety and the safety of others, including parties for whom they have a professional responsibility.

To the fullest extent of the law, neither the Publisher nor the authors, contributors, or editors, assume any liability for any injury and/or damage to persons or property as a matter of products liability, negligence or otherwise, or from any use or operation of any methods, products, instructions, or ideas contained in the material herein.

**Library of Congress Cataloging-in-Publication Data**
A catalog record for this book is available from the Library of Congress

**British Library Cataloguing-in-Publication Data**
A catalogue record for this book is available from the British Library

ISBN: 978-0-12-800959-8

For information on all MK publications
visit our website at **store.elsevier.com**

This book has been manufactured using Print On Demand technology. Each copy is produced to order and is limited to black ink. The online version of this book will show color figures where appropriate.

# DEDICATION AND THANKS

This book is dedicated to the One who started all processes by proclaiming, "Let there be light!"

Thanks to the following individuals who helped review my book:

- Chris Finden-Browne
- William Powell
- Tim Rogers
- Phil Withers

# AUTHOR'S INFORMATION

**John Long** is a process architect who has worked in the banking, energy, software, telecommunications, defense, and research industries. He has a Master of Science in Computer Science from the University of Tennessee. He has published two other professional books:

- ITIL® Version 3 at a Glance: Information Quick Reference
- ITIL® 2011 At a Glance

He has also self-published a number of other books. He has a terrific wife of 26 years, with whom he enjoys spending time now that all four of his children are out of the house. He can be reached at johnoflong@gmail.com.

# CONTENTS

# ABSTRACT

Process modeling often seems simple enough. How hard can it be to create a workflow diagram? After decades of creating and reviewing process models, it has become clear to the author that there are good practices and bad practices. These practices greatly influence how their models are interpreted and understood. Modelers need guidance for the "style" of their models. This style includes many different style elements that focus on structure, relationships, consistency, and identification. You may find that some of these style elements do not work for you. Some style elements also might not work with your tooling. Adopt the style elements that work for your team. By starting with awareness of all of these leading practices and making conscious decisions regarding which to adopt or not, your projects will avoid the common pitfalls in process modeling.

# INTRODUCTION

## I.1 WHY A STYLE BOOK ON PROCESS MODELING?

Process modeling is a leading practice that has been growing in importance for organizations pursuing increased operating efficiencies. Established process-based capabilities become repeatable, training becomes easier, quality is improved, and process outcomes are more reliable. Many businesses and enterprises look at their processes for a number of reasons:

- To understand all functions that are performed within the business
- To understand the context for proposed solutions within the business
- To understand how to improve the performance of the business

As a result of the increasing interest in process models and process modeling, there are many process models, and results are often very disjoint. A process model created in one project often is not compatible with processes from a different project. The result is processes that do not work well together, wasted effort, rework, inefficiency, and delayed organizational benefits from improved processes.

This is similar to the confusion within software design decades ago. There were different ways to create design models, and everyone had their favorites. If you had to integrate systems with different types of designs, you had to spend considerable effort understanding those differences and reconfiguring the software and systems. The advent of the Unified Modeling Language (UML) greatly reduced that. Now, many designers can look at and understand design models from other teams because of their adherence to UML. (Of course, many people still use other non-UML approaches, and UML is not without its limitations.) The general effect is predictable and beneficial.

By standardizing on the form and format, developers have a constraint. All new designs must be expressed within the constraint of the UML.

Having a standard constraint for the format forces developers to innovate in other areas. Innovation in the format is a nonvaluable innovation and in fact reduces interoperability with other solutions. Innovation in function, reliability, security, or other aspects is valuable and that value is enhanced by having improved interoperability with other solutions.

The process modeling world thus far has been in a chaotic state. There are many different ways to produce process models. In Chapter 2, I will describe some of the different notations that exist. Although there has been some convergence within the industry, there is still disagreement on whether converging is the right thing to do. For example, Business Process Modeling Notation (BPMN) is a standard process modeling notation created by the Object Management Group (OMG), the same organization that manages UML. Unfortunately, not all modeling tools use BPMN, and those that claim to use BPMN do not necessarily adhere to the entire standard.

Thus, we're still in a bit of a Wild West situation concerning process modeling. This nonstandardized environment reduces overall efficiency, interoperability, time to value, and total value realization for new solutions. Industry standardization may one day reach Process Modeling, but until then, organizations should adopt standards internally for their own benefit. This publication will provide the information these organizations should be aware of as they seek process modeling standardization and the resulting efficiencies and improved time to value for new solutions.

## I.2 A LOT OF PEOPLE JUST ARE NOT "PROCESS PEOPLE"

The other day, I ran across the workflow shown in Figure I.1. It was created by people who were serious about their work, but it was not a serious workflow. It contained numerous problems, including:

- The flow of work sometimes went backward. Note the arrows that are two sided.
- The flow of work appears to start multiple threads at the same time. Is the task entitled "Payment received" supposed to be a decision, or two parallel threads that occur simultaneously? The time required to clarify this confusion delays time to value.

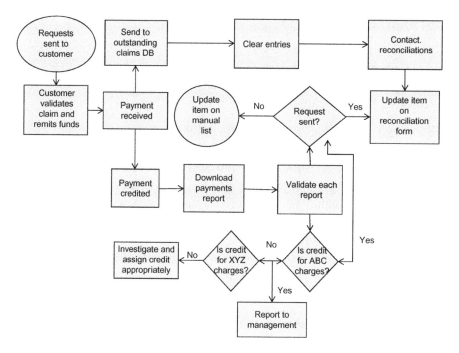

*Figure I.1 A recent bad example of style.*

- It's difficult to tell where the workflow stops. Note that circles are sometimes used to indicate the end of a flow, but not always. Does the designation of a circle mean something or not? The confusion delays enterprise adoption and time to value.
- What do the task labels mean? Would everyone in their organization understand the workflow with such cryptic information?
- What is taking place in the connection to the box labeled "Report to Management"? Is that coming from one of the decisions above it?

This example reminded me that not everyone actually "gets" what a workflow is. Anyone can draw boxes with arrows between them. But there aren't that many who can draw such diagrams so that they represent a flow of work that is consistent, understandable, and can be followed.

I have seen many people be given the responsibility of creating a process workflow, and I have seen many bad results. I hope that this book will help transform well-intentioned process modelers into better process modelers that deliver organization value more quickly.

## I.3 THE NEED FOR STYLE

When an organization selects a specific tool set for creating process models, there will still be significant ways to vary how processes are described. For instance, BPMN specifies how tasks look, but there are no rules on the following:

- How tasks are named: If I call a task "Print Report," will that clash with other tasks that basically do the same thing?
- How big a task is: Should "Design Software" be considered a task, or is that something larger than a task, like a process? Should a task called "Enter Data" be considered a task, or is too small to be a task? If a task in a workflow encompasses work passed to multiple people, is it really a task?
- How tasks relate to roles: How do I indicate whether other roles can participate in a task? Can more than one role be responsible for a task?

Modeling teams need guidance for the "style" of their models. The style includes many different characteristics that help different process elements appear to be part of an integrated and fully interoperable system. This includes:

- Naming and numbering
- Structure
- Relationships

This book provides a "style" for process modeling that I have developed based on my experience over the past 25 years in many projects, in many organizations. Based on the results that I have been able to assess after the projects have ended, I have concluded that there are in fact core leading practices that enable projects to produce value more efficiently. Projects that do not adopt these practices will tend to have waste, rework, and delayed time to value. This style includes many "style elements," which include leading practices, rules, or conventions to adhere to. You may find that some of these style elements do not work for you. Some style elements also might not work with your tooling. Adopt the style elements that work for your team. Use the appendix at the back to identify which style elements your team will use. By starting with awareness of all of these leading practices and making conscious decisions regarding which to adopt or not, your projects will avoid the common pitfalls in process modeling and time to value.

## I.4 THE NEED FOR ACCURACY AND DETAIL

Figure I.2 shows a high-level view of how to drive from New York City to Los Angeles. It does not give any details. It does not tell which roads to take or how long you will be on any of those roads. It may correctly indicate how you would get from New York to Los Angeles, but you would never actually use this map to drive that route. It is too general. Plus, it is not accurate. There is no road you could take that would be a straight line from New York City to Los Angeles. Thus, it is neither accurate, nor detailed, nor valuable. However, if you want to simply indicate someone going from one city to the next, it might be sufficient.

Now look at the next map in Figure I.3. This map is accurate. The route in the map is indeed a route you could take from New York City to Los Angeles because it is generated from underlying detail that includes roads that matched a standard description and where adopted into the model. This depiction does not have sufficient detail to actually use it to drive the distance. However, it is useful to show that it could be done and that the details for how to do it are within the underlying model.

*Figure I.2 High-level map with little detail.*

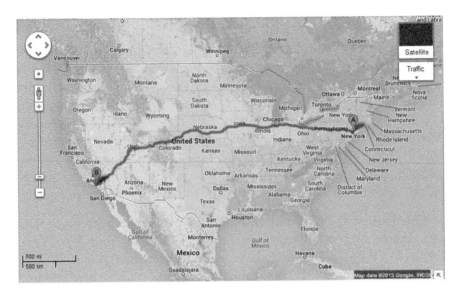

*Figure I.3 High-level map with more detail.*

Figure I.4 is a detailed map going from New York City to Los Angeles. This shows the sequence and distances required to drive the route. It goes on for many pages, and it's hard to look at it in detail all at once. However, it is both accurate and detailed.

Processes are like maps. They show how to go from one place (where something has been done) to another place (where something needs to be done). Processes can be accurate and/or detailed. However, many processes are created without accuracy or detail. Figure I.5 is one such example.

In this example, there are blocks that seem to represent tasks within a process, but it's not clear how they relate. There are a number of questions about this model:

- Are these performed sequentially, from left-to-right or top-to-bottom?
- Assuming this is left-to-right, why does Update Work Environment Design seem to stop before Update and Assign Resources to Teams? What is the significance of that? Or was it just a diagramming error?
- What does the Confirm task mean? Confirm what?
- What does the Update task mean? Update what?

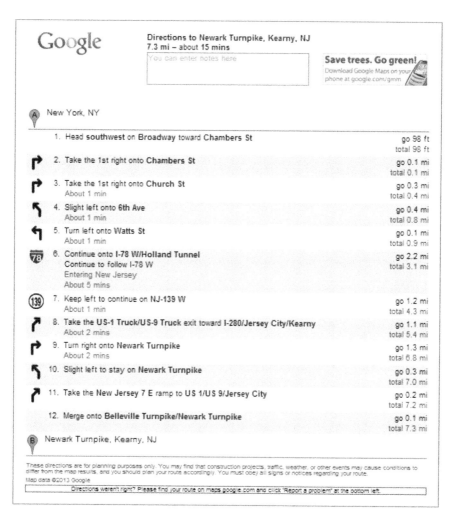

*Figure I.4 Low-level detail.*

- Why is Confirm smaller than Update? Does that mean one task is larger and more involved than the other?

  This confusion causes delays in adoption, execution, and time to value.

  Figure I.6 is another example. There is a sense of a workflow, but it's not very clear. Questions concerning this diagram include:

- Why are there arrows that go back and forth between the Perform, Maintain, and Identify tasks? Are these performed as part of a loop?

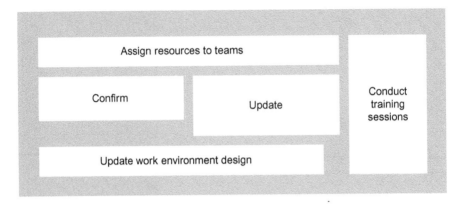

*Figure I.5 High-level process diagram.*

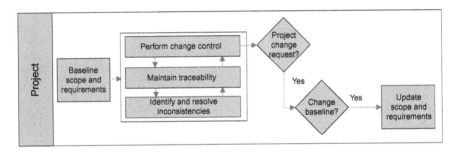

*Figure I.6 Low-level process diagram.*

- How do you go from Perform Change Control to Project Change Request?
- What happens if you reach a "no" decision for either Project Change Request or Change Baseline?

Although there is greater detail in this workflow, it is not accurate and will cause delays in adoption, execution, and time to value.

In both cases, it is hard to follow the processes because they are either not detailed enough or not accurate. Most people would never embark on a trip without a sufficiently detailed and accurate map, yet people embark every day on work without sufficiently detailed and accurate process models. No wonder some organizations flounder when it comes to process and routinely experience scrap, rework, and delays in time to value.

## I.5 TOWARD A PROCESS ARCHITECTURE

As your business defines an increasing number of process models, these models will begin to represent more and more of your business. Taken as a whole, these business process models constitute the process architecture of the business. Just as there is information architecture, application architecture, and other architectures within the business, process architecture identifies the various business processes and their relationships.

Your business should take care to maintain and improve these models over time because they are the only models that describe what the organization actually does. All of the other architectures are supporting systems, applications, information, or facilities that the resources "doing" the work of the business use. Because they represent business capabilities, processes are the most valuable assets to the business. As your business capabilities expand and improve, you should also expand and improve your process architecture.

A well-crafted architecture of any type will be composed of parts that integrate and fit well together. For this reason, your processes need to follow a standard modeling style for your organization. This style must include all of the leading practices that you have either created or adopted. It is very important that your process modeling projects follow a standard style to avoid scrap, rework, waste, delayed time to value and additional reconfiguration efforts that would be required to enhance interoperability and enhanced value.

## I.6 WHAT THIS BOOK IS NOT

This book is oriented toward the process modeling practitioner who is looking for better ways to define, manage, and organize business processes. It is *not* a book to do any of the following:

- Help you sell the idea of business process modeling in your organization. There are plenty of books already on the market that are oriented toward management and executives on this topic.
- Give you a primer on how to do process modeling. It is assumed that you are already modeling and are now looking for style guide standards.

- Tell you which software and tools you should be using. The style in the book will work with different tools.

You will find several good ideas in this book. I also hope that you will share your own good ideas with me so I might be able to update and improve this book in the future.

## I.7 IN SUMMARY

Process modelers and process modeling organizations should define a style of modeling that will result in informative, high quality, and integrated processes. The work performed along these lines will yield process models that will reduce scrap, rework, and waste and improve adoption and time to value from the developed processes.

# CHAPTER 1

# Eight of the Biggest Process Modeling Problems

Process modeling projects are not always a success. They can often suffer from many of the same maladies that make other types of projects fail. However, there are specific errors that process modeling projects can fall prey to. The following sections describe some of those errors.

## 1.1 NOT FOCUSING ON THE DIAGRAMS

Process models are a balance of workflow diagrams and descriptions of workflows. Workflow diagrams are the most powerful and expressive aspect of process models. The diagrams are the first thing that everyone wants to see and it is the diagrams that provide the construct for their understanding of the text. The workflow diagrams, in a very small space, convey tasks, sequencing, decisions, participation, and information. If a picture is worth a 1000 words, then complex workflow diagrams are the equivalent of, perhaps not exactly 1000 words, but at least several hundred. Modeling projects should exercise rigor in the creation of workflow diagrams because those diagrams are the expressive artifacts within the project. By "rigor," I mean that workflows should actually follow logic, be consistent, and tell the story of how something happens. Some projects are careless in how they create workflow diagrams, and upon review, the diagrams don't hold up.

## 1.2 ONLY FOCUSING ON THE WORKFLOW DIAGRAMS

On the other hand, process models do not rely on diagrams alone. Although diagrams are the most powerful aspect of a process modeling project, text and prose are very important as well. Text is really the only way to provide detailed descriptions of roles, work products, activities, and tasks. In addition, textual annotations are important additions to a workflow diagram to help elaborate upon what is happening within a workflow. The textual descriptions, when integrated well, help tell an overall story of the processes you model.

## 1.3 IGNORING THE PROCESS ARCHITECTURE

A collection of processes defined by a business need to be crafted into an overall process architecture. This is not always easy, primarily because business processes are often done individually or in small projects, resulting in processes with the following characteristics:

- Unevenness, representing different levels of complexity
- Overlapping scope, with starting and stopping points that go over the same space
- Heterogeneous, with different process attributes

The resulting collection of processes will be difficult to use together. You may have to do a lot of redesigning and refactoring of the processes in order to make them usable together.

## 1.4 IGNORING PROCESS INTERFACES

As mentioned elsewhere in this book, processes rarely operate in a vacuum. Often, one process is only one cog in an entire mechanism that makes up a business. The work that is done by one process is almost always used by other processes to do their work.

For example, Customer Relationship Management (CRM) processes create market analysis reports that are used by marketing processes to forecast sales for an upcoming period. Product management processes use those forecasts to make decisions on whether to increase or decrease development activity. Portfolio management processes use those decisions to spawn new development processes. And it goes on and on.

Therefore, it makes sense to focus on the processes that interface with the processes you are working on. Even if those processes are out of scope for your modeling project, it is important to be aware of what processes are related to the ones you are modeling. Failure to identify process interfaces give a false sense that only the processes you are modeling are of any importance. This false understanding may give you tactical success, but it ultimately hurts the business.

## 1.5 INCONSISTENT OR NONSTANDARD NOTATION

Too many projects are started without an agreement beforehand of the notation to be used. "Just start modeling," they will say. "We'll work out inconsistencies later."

Of course, no one would tell programmers to just start writing code without first agreeing on the programming language to use. Technical writers would not start writing unless they first agreed upon the document template they would use. Software architects would not start envisioning the architecture unless they first understood the basic architectural and technical constraints they had to work with.

Yet, unfortunately, well-meaning managers who are inexperienced in process modeling projects just tell modelers to use whatever template or stencil they want from their favorite desktop drawing tool. This always leads to different workers defending their notation as the best one, causing team confusion and conflict. It is best to just nip that one in the bud at the beginning of the project. The lead architect of a project or the lead modeler of the modeling team should establish the practices to be followed. Failing to establish these standards at the beginning of the work will always cause scrap, rework, and delayed time to value.

## 1.6 MAKING OVERLY COMPLICATED WORKFLOWS

Processes typically have interfaces with other processes, but they also have secondary effects on other processes. With process interfaces, one process actually passes a work product to another process. However, a process may also have an effect on other processes even if it does not specifically pass a work product to those processes. When this distinction is not made, workflow diagrams can become a confusing jumble of connections from one process or activity to another. The workflow ends up justifying any connection between any two parts of a workflow. This leaves implementers in a quandary, wondering how to implement it all. This is described in more detail in Section 9.5.

Another way a project can end up with overly complicated workflows is to identify any and all exceptions within a workflow. Workflows should start out with the "sunny day" workflow that indicates what happens when everything is working correctly. After that, the modeler should begin to add primary exceptions to the workflow that describe what happens when things do not go as planned. However, it is possible to model too many exceptions. In actuality, any process, no matter how automated, can be interrupted at any time and go in a different direction, but the value of modeling any and every exception is small. It is best to focus on the most important exceptions to a workflow.

## 1.7 FOCUSING ON JOBS, NOT ROLES

Many organizations have a difficult time differentiating between roles and jobs. The differences can sometimes be subtle. When that happens, roles become jobs, and jobs become organizations. Tying a process to an organization can be problematic for a number of reasons.

First, organization-centric workflows can be used to justify the reason for an organization's existence. The workflows can cause the stakeholders to focus on what the organization does rather than the work itself (whether current or target state). Instead of enabling organizational efficiency analysis, the workflows may help an organization further entrench itself in its behavior. The modeling becomes protective of an organization rather than helping the business improve its efficiency and effectiveness. Instead, a business should identify roles divorced from organizational ties.

Second, organization-centric workflows can restrict the thinking of the organization. Instead of thinking about the types of skills that will be required within the various roles executing a workflow, the organization may try to force-fit the workflow within the mission of an existing organization. The organization must be able to freely think about changing its organizational structure and organizational purpose in order to create a viable and long-lasting set of organizational processes.

## 1.8 FUZZY WORK PRODUCTS

Workflows produce outputs. Those outputs are the results of real work that is performed. And those outputs, in turn, tend to be inputs into other work. Inputs and outputs are information work products. As such, these information work products should be defined in sufficient detail to provide guidance for a workflow. If a workflow does not have its work products clearly understood, then that workflow does not know what it is producing, nor does it know what it is consuming.

Sometimes, a process modeling project can concentrate so much effort on getting the flow of work correct that work products become ill-defined. Ill-defined work products may result in:

- Work products that are not tangible
- Work products that are ill-defined
- Fewer work products than are really needed
- Workflows that cannot be executed because no one knows what information is to be produced or received.

When a project allows "fuzzy work products" to exist, the implementers will have to do more work. It slows down implementation and there is a delay in time to value. Thus, fuzzy work products should be avoided. Take the time to define work products in sufficient detail so development will not be delayed.

# CHAPTER 2

# Selecting a Notation

To model processes, you have to select a modeling notation. By selecting a standard notation, you establish a standard way of creating your diagrams and a standard approach for integrating the work of multiple process modelers.

## 2.1 THE RIGHT NOTATION FOR YOU

The beginning of every modeling project should start with a review of the real goals of the effort and the various notation schemes that might apply.

Let me state up front that I have a preference for notation. I think Business Process Modeling Notation (BPMN) is the best notation for process modeling at this time. There are a number of advantages that I will describe later in this chapter. However, not all projects will use BPMN. There are a number of reasons for that, including:

- The sponsors of your project insist on using a different notation
- The modeling tool that you are using requires a different notation
- There is a large number of legacy models that you must integrate with that use a different notation

So, the right notation for your project is the one that works best for you. It is better to review the notation options prior to starting the work to avoid the scrap, rework, and delayed time to value that arises when notation standards are adjusted throughout a project. Nevertheless, here is a brief summary of some process modeling notation that is currently being used. This is not intended to be an exhaustive list.

## 2.2 FLOWCHARTS

Flowchart notation is probably the most used notation for process models. Most people understand it. It's simple. Most tools provide some variation of it.

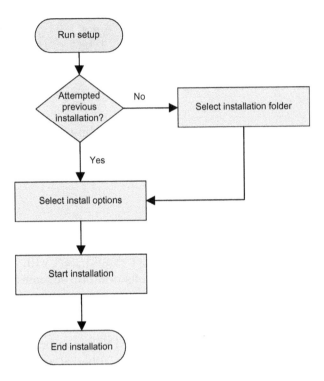

*Figure 2.1 Flowchart example.*

The problem with flowcharts is that many people add additional constructs to flowcharts to be more expressive. Here are some common constructs that are added:

- Swim lanes
- Parallel tasks
- Linkages to tools or databases
- Complex decision nodes that allow more than yes/no answers

Flowchart notation is also where you will find the most variation between practitioners. If you choose flowchart notation, you will have to agree, as a team, which constructs are in and which ones are out. An example is shown in Figure 2.1.

## 2.3 BUSINESS PROCESS MODELING NOTATION

BPMN was created by a consortium of businesses under the oversight of the Object Management Group (OMG). It uses a basic flowchart style

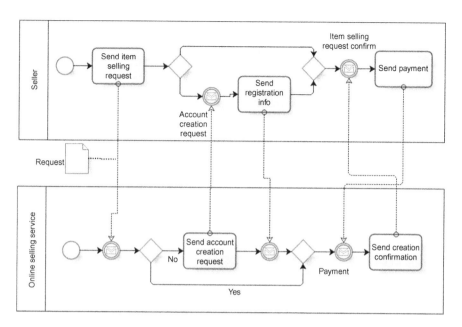

*Figure 2.2 BPMN example.*

of notation heavily augmented with other constructs for parallel tasks, complex decisions, events, start and stop nodes, swim lanes, and others. The notation is very expressive and actually allows your diagrams to be a bit smaller than regular flowcharts, depending on the complexity of the process. It turns out that the more complex the process, the more advantage you have using BPMN rather than normal flowchart notation.

There is a great deal of flexibility concerning the use of BPMN. You can make simple process models or very detailed process models. You can use swim lanes or not. You can make your diagrams vertical or horizontal. Even if you adopt this standard, there will still be a need to specify the modeling style of your group.

Not all tool vendors have moved over to BPMN. They are probably waiting to see if it is actually going to be a hit or not. Not all standards promoted by the OMG become popular. An example is shown in Figure 2.2.

## 2.4 LINE OF VISIBILITY ENTERPRISE MODELING

LOVEM stands for Line of Visibility Enterprise Modeling (or sometimes Line of Visibility Engineering Method). LOVEM was created by

IBM to model workflows. It uses basic flowchart notation with horizontal swim lanes. The top swim lane is always used to represent the customer or end user. Items in each workflow "swim lane" below the customer line have "visibility" to that specific role in that specific swim lane. Interactions with the customer or other swim lanes are indicated by a dashed line. These interactions should be described as to what information is exchanged and the business rules governing that exchange. Anything in the end user/customer swim lane represents a "moment of truth" because it is the critical point of customer interaction point in that workflow. Those items are critical interactions with specific information. The bottom two swim lanes represent data and tools (automation). The workflow links to the data swim lane show input to, or output from, data repositories. (Some practitioners leave out the data swim lane.) The workflow links to the tools swim lane show interaction with tools. An example is shown in Figure 2.3.

LOVEM diagrams provide information necessary for implementation because they establish the very useful graphical basis to begin the design of the roles, tools and information work products used by each of the roles and tools. These diagrams can be a happy medium between the simplicity needed for high-level consumers of process models and the detail needed for low-level implementers of the process.

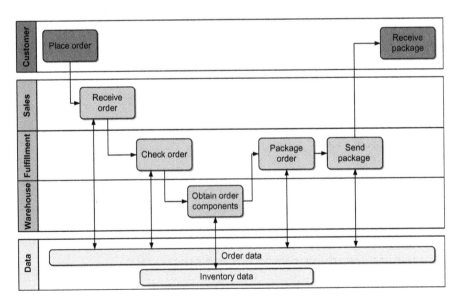

*Figure 2.3 LOVEM example.*

However, it may be too detailed for the high-level users and not detailed enough for the implementers. It should be noted that most BPMN tools are focused around process modeling and provide additional capabilities to record information about roles, work products, and supporting information necessary for describing processes.

## 2.5 USE CASES

The term "use case" is one of the most overused terms in software engineering. It means many things to many people. Those who are well versed in Unified Modeling Language (UML) (Section 2.6) know that use case notation specifies certain constructs. These constructs include ovals for use cases, stick figures for actors (not roles), and connections between actors, use cases, and other use cases.

This seems to be lost on many people who have co-opted the term "use case" to mean "how to do something." We will ignore this very ambiguous meaning and instead concentrate on the more specific use case notation that is specified by UML.

I have used use cases to describe processes but they do not work very well. Use cases are good for showing what basic functions are carried out by a system or solution, but they often fail to indicate sequencing, parallel processing, decision-making, or the start and completion of a process. One might use a use case diagram to show the high-level set of processes that take place within a system, but that may be its only real use in process modeling. An example is shown in Figure 2.4.

## 2.6 UML

There are constructs in UML that could be used to model processes. The most prominent of these is the activity diagram, as shown in Figure 2.5. These are vertical diagrams, using swim lanes and flowchart-like notation. They also use horizontal bars to coordinate the initiation and completion of task threads. In addition, there are start and stop nodes. These diagrams are an improvement on normal flowcharts.

If you must use UML, activity diagrams are the best for modeling processes. However, many UML tools do not provide the additional capabilities for recording information about work products and roles that are necessary for creating good process documentation. If you

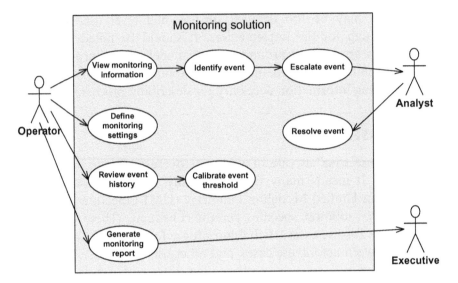

*Figure 2.4 Use case diagram example.*

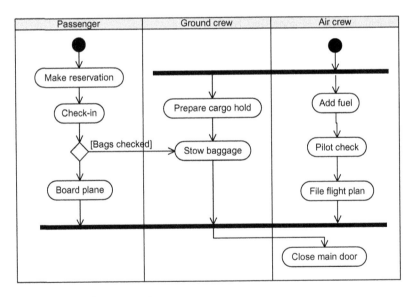

*Figure 2.5 UML activity diagram example.*

must use UML, you may have to take UML diagrams into other tools such as MS Word to add the additional content.

Another type of UML diagram is the sequence diagram. These diagrams are accurate, show sequence and precedence, and when things

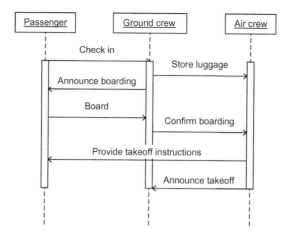

*Figure 2.6 UML sequence diagram example.*

start and stop. Unfortunately, they are just a little difficult for the non-initiated to understand. If you show these diagrams to high-level subject-matter experts (SMEs) to validate a process, you will get a lot of blank stares. These diagrams tend to work with software engineers, but not with SMEs. It is recommended that you do not use sequence diagrams unless you are working with people who already know UML. An example is shown in Figure 2.6.

## 2.7 IDEF0

Icam Definition for Function Modeling (IDEF0) is a notation used for modeling functions, typically the functions of a system. They can also be used to model the functions of a business. At first blush, they appear to be fairly simple flow diagrams like a very simple flowchart diagram. However, they are really diagrams that show the flow of information and data between functions. Process models should show the flow of work between the parts of a process. Instead, IDEF0 shows the flow of data and information. There is an important difference here. In an IDEF0 diagram, information may flow into a function but not used until some other triggering event occurs. The triggering event may be the flow of some information, but it is not indicated in the diagram. An example is shown in Figure 2.7.

There are three types of information in an IDEF0 diagram:

1. Inputs, which always flow into the left-hand side of a function box. Inputs are transformed into outputs.

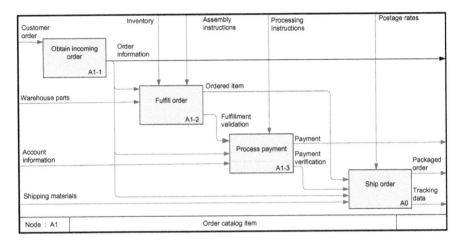

*Figure 2.7 IDEF0 diagram example.*

2. Outputs, which always flow out of the right-hand side of a function box. Outputs are created typically from inputs, using guidance from controls.
3. Controls, which always flow into the top of a function box. Controls represent reference material that is used to carry out the work and are a kind of indirect input.

Because IDEF0 diagrams show where ALL information goes, the diagrams tend to be very busy. They are very useful for showing where all information is coming and going, but they are not good for showing the flow of work. IDEF0 process models are independent of organization, tools, and roles. These diagrams are only recommended for reference models for the information that passes through processes (Figure 2.7).

# CHAPTER 3

# Process Modeling Goals

When you begin a process modeling project, it is important to define specific determining features of the project. The modeler should understand in a clear way who or what will need to change as a result of the modeling action and what the goal is for that change. This includes purpose, scope, depth, and degree of automation.

## 3.1 PURPOSE

The purpose of the project is the most important, and it guides how you conduct the project. This purpose may include, but is not restricted to, the following:

- Understanding how the business currently works
- Bringing some sense of formality and repeatability to immature processes
- Planning how a part of the business should work
- Looking for efficiencies in existing processes
- Designing the context in which a new IT system should work
- Strategic planning

There should be a primary purpose, although there may be secondary purposes. The primary purpose helps you to narrow how much of the business to include in the effort as well as the degree of detail you will need to complete the work.

## 3.2 SCOPE

The scope of the project, as with any project, puts boundaries around the subject to be modeled. However, in a process modeling project, you need to determine whether you will model the current state, the target state, or both. The following table can help determine your scope based on your purpose.

| Purpose | Current State | Target State |
|---|---|---|
| Understanding how the business currently works | Yes | |
| Bringing a sense of formality and repeatability to immature processes | Yes | Yes |
| Planning how a part of the business should work | | Yes |
| Looking for efficiencies in existing processes | Yes | Yes |
| Designing the context in which a new IT system should work | | Yes |
| Strategic planning | | Yes |

## 3.3 DEPTH

The depth of a modeling project is the degree of detail that you will need in your models. Process models typically start with very little detail and with a lot of abstraction. As you understand more about a process, you can add more detail to a process and decompose each workflow into smaller activities and tasks. However, not all projects need the same degree of detail. Projects that have a strategic focus will not need to be decomposed into much detail, whereas projects that model processes that must be designed and implemented will need much more detail and decomposition.

## 3.4 DEGREE OF AUTOMATION

The goals of a process modeling project typically include increasing the automation of those processes. When you define your project goals, you should understand how much additional automation is needed. This may involve simply expanding upon work that is already partially automated. Or, at the other end of the spectrum, the project may involve automation of an entire workflow due to the introduction of new systems. Automation reduces cost, risk, and performance variance by eliminating or reducing human effort. It enables enhanced monitoring, variance detection and control, and can increase quality as a result. Automation can increase performance by removing bottlenecks and increasing the speed with which specific tasks can be executed.

The amount of automation that is involved affects how you model the project. First, increased automation changes the roles that perform specific activities and tasks. This may reduce the involvement of some roles in your processes or may free those roles up to do other types of work.

As automation is increased in your business processes, existing workflows may take on a different nature. In other words, the tasks that are performed and their sequencing may be changed when a work-flow is automated. For instance, there may need to be additional tasks for data preparation or for obtaining data from other systems. Another possibility may include combining tasks that were formerly performed separately when they were not automated.

However, one of the biggest aspects to automation is the additional functionality that comes with the inclusion of new automation systems. When a new system is used to automate a workflow that new system often brings with it new functionality that project sponsors will typically want to harness as well. This means new subprocesses, activities, and tasks may be added to the project scope.

# CHAPTER 4

# Defining Processes and Process Elements

This section defines what a "process" is, as well as the components that make up a process. The components that make of a process are called "process elements."

## 4.1 PROCESS

A process is an organized collection of tasks that together accomplish a specific objective. These tasks are organized in activities and sequenced into workflows. Roles accomplish tasks, transforming inputs into outputs. A process may define policies, standards, and procedures as needed.

A process should be defined by the following items:

- Title: Provide a brief name of the process. See Section 7.4.
- ID: Provide the identifier specific to this process. See Chapter 8.
- Description: Provide a summarization of what takes place within the process. This can be just a few sentences or several paragraphs. If a lengthier description is needed, the description should link to a document that describes the process in more detail.
- Scope: A description of what is included in the process and what is not included in the process. This is necessary because a process name often conjures up different ideas about what that process is. For instance, a "Change Management" process may mean different things depending on whether it means changes to a business, changes to a system under development, or changes to IT operations.
- How it starts: Describe the events that cause the workflow to start. There may be different types of events that start the workflow, such as user action, errors, and form submission.
- Workflow
  - Workflow diagram: A picture is worth a thousand words, and so a well-crafted workflow diagram provides a wealth of information to your readers. Use the right notation for your stakeholders. See Chapter 2.

- Workflow description: Optionally, provide a textual description of the workflow diagram to provide greater clarity.
- Activities: List all of the activities in the process.
- Roles: List all of the roles involved in the process. Because roles participate in different ways, you may want to identify how each role participates (see Section 10.4).
- Work products: List all of the work products involved in the process. This includes inputs, outputs, and controls (see Section 9.6).
- How it ends: Describe the situations in which the workflow comes to an end or transfers workflow to another process.
- Interfaces: Typically, processes send work (and outputs) to other processes. In addition, inputs may come to this process from other processes. List all interfaces with other processes, including inputs and outputs. The interface description should identify which activity in this process interfaces with which activity in another process. (see Chapter 9).
- Outcomes: In nonwork product terms, describe what is accomplished by the process. In other words, for a Change Management process, do not say an outcome is a Change Order. Instead, say that the outcome is a change that has been categorized, approved, implemented, and tested.

## 4.2 ACTIVITY

An activity is a collection of related tasks. Tasks are grouped into an activity, and activities are grouped into a process.

An activity should be defined by the following items:

- Title: Provide a brief name of the activity (see Section 7.5).
- ID: Provide the identifier specific to this activity. See Chapter 8.
- Description: Provide a summarization of what takes place within the activity. This can be just a few sentences or several paragraphs. If a lengthier description is needed, the description should link to a document that describes the activity in more detail.
- Workflow
  - Workflow diagram: This should be the same notation as that used by a process workflow.
  - Workflow description: Optionally, provide a textual description of the workflow diagram to provide greater clarity.

- Tasks: List all of the tasks in the activity.
- Roles: List all of the roles involved in the activity. Because roles participate in different ways, you may want to identify how each role participates (see Section 10.4).
- Work products: List all of the work products involved in the activity. This includes inputs, outputs, and controls (see Section 9.6).

## 4.3 TASK

A task is a unit of work performed by a role. Typically, I don't decompose a workflow below the task level.

A task should be defined by the following items:

- Title: Provide a brief name of the task (see Section 7.5).
- ID: Provide the identifier specific to this task. See Chapter 8.
- Description: Provide a summarization of what takes place within the task. This can be just a few sentences or several paragraphs. If a lengthier description is needed, the description should link to a document that describes the activity in more detail.
- Workflow
  - Workflow diagram: This should be the same notation as that used by a process workflow.
  - Workflow description: Optionally, provide a textual description of the workflow diagram to provide greater clarity.
- Procedures: List all of the detailed procedures used in this task. Each procedure is a documented series of steps to be carried out in support of this task. There may be multiple procedures. There may be no procedures.
- Roles: List all of the roles involved in the task. Because roles participate in different ways, you may want to identify how each role participates (see Section 10.4).
- Work products: List all of the work products involved in the task. This includes inputs, outputs, and controls (see Section 9.6).

## 4.4 PROCEDURE

A procedure is a detailed series of steps that a single role performs to complete low-level work. A procedure is defined simply by the sequence of steps to be carried out.

## 4.5 ROLE

A role is a part that is played by a system, individual, or organization. Each role should be defined by the following items:

- Title: Provide a brief name of the role (see Section 7.7).
- ID: Provide the identifier specific to this role (see Chapter 8).
- Description: Provide a summarization of what the role does.
- Processes, activities, and tasks: List each process, activity, and task in which the role participates. This may be in the form of a Responsible, Accountable, Communicating, and Informed (RACI) Chart.
- Work products: List each work product that this role helps produce, whether the role is specifically responsible for the work product or just participates in its creation.

## 4.6 WORK PRODUCT

A tangible result of work, typically a document, but could also include code, digital media, hardware, or similar outputs. Work products include both artifacts (items produced during development that only have value for the development team) and deliverables (items produced during development that have value to the end user or customer).

A work product should be defined by the following items:

- Title: Provide a brief name of the work product (see Section 7.7).
- ID: Provide the identifier specific to this work product. See Chapter 8.
- Description: Provide a summarization of what the work product contains.
- Processes, activities, and tasks: List each process, activity, and task in which the work product is an input, output, or control. Specify whether the work product is an input, output, or control.
- Roles: List each role that is involved in the creation or modification of the work product.

# CHAPTER 5

# Process Structure

## 5.1 WORKFLOW DECOMPOSITION

The term "process," in a generic sense, can apply to very large things such as managing an IT organization or to very small things such as how to install a DVD drive in your laptop. From a generic viewpoint, a "process" can be anything that involves a workflow. However, this view of a process can lead to a lot of confusion. When you discuss the "processes" with other people, they may have widely divergent views on the size and complexity of the processes you are talking about. A process may contain other processes, which themselves may contain other processes.

For this reason, people need a way to distinguish between large workflows and small, detailed workflows. Here is a fairly simple approach:

- A process is an end to end workflow, made up of a series of logical activities that can be owned by a single managerial stakeholder. It is something to which a stakeholder will be held accountable. For instance, Change Management is typically a process within an organization.
- A process activity contains many tasks. Tasks are unit of work that can be done by a single role. A task within the Change Management process may be "Fill out Change Request" or "Assign Change Request."
- Because it is hard to show all process tasks within a single diagram/model, it is useful to group tasks into activities. In some cases, it may be useful to have activities within activities. For instance, "Evaluate Change Request" is typically an activity within Change Management and includes several tasks.
- The specifics of how to carry out a task are described in a procedure. For instance, there may be a procedure called "Fill out Change Request in Change Request Tool" that is associated with the "Fill out Change Request" task.

Thus, the decomposition of a process is as follows:

- A process is composed of
  - Activities, which are composed of
    - Tasks, which are completed by following
      - Procedures

## 5.2 THE COMPONENTS OF A WORKFLOW DIAGRAM

A workflow diagram should contain the following:

- One or more start nodes that indicate how the workflow is initiated. Without a start node, it may be difficult to determine what caused the workflow to begin.
- One or more stop nodes that indicate how the workflow is terminated. Without a stop node, it may be difficult to determine if the workflow was simply left unfinished.
- Two or more activities or tasks. A workflow should not have just a single activity or task because such a workflow does not require decomposition and has no real value.
- Connections between tasks. These connections represent the directional flow of work between activities or tasks, not the flow of information, although information is typically passed with the flow of work. (The arrows indicate the direction of the flow.) For instance, in Change Management, when modeling the submission of a change request, you would want to show a connection between "Submit Change Request" and "Accept Change Request." The Accept Change Request task, when being performed, may use additional information to carry out the task, like a Change Request Database or User Information, but the flow of work is clearly caused by sending the change request, not the user information from whatever repository it may reside in.

In addition, workflows may optionally contain the following:

- Decision nodes: Typically shown as diamond boxes, decision nodes are used to show the different paths that result from a decision. Yes/no decisions are the most basic, but more complex decision nodes that show multiple decision results are also necessary.
- Synchronization bars or nodes: Some tasks must be carried out in parallel and may not proceed until all parallel tasks have been

completed. For these situations, use synchronization bars or nodes to show the beginning of parallel tasks and the end of parallel tasks.

- Comment boxes: These are informative devices that can be used anywhere in a workflow diagram to provide clarity about what is happening in a workflow. For instance, a comment box may provide clarity for the conditions in which a workflow is started or to describe more detail about a decision box.
- Interfaces with other activities or processes: Rarely are processes self-contained. Most processes interface with other processes because the output of a process is typically used by some other process. These interfaces should be indicated with a special symbol. In addition, within a process, the workflow within an activity typically interfaces with the workflow in another activity that belongs to the same process. These interfaces should be shown as well.

Figure 5.1 illustrates these process elements.

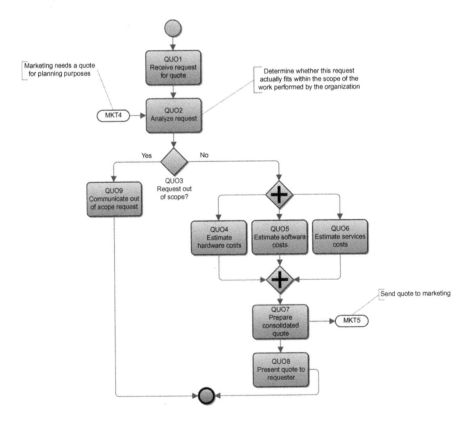

*Figure 5.1 Workflow components example.*

## 5.3 THE VALUE OF SWIM LANES

Many process modelers like swim lanes because it is possible to show both the flow of work with the roles who carry out the parts of a process. This seems simple until you realize the complexity of what it means to "perform" an activity or task.

In Figure 5.2, there are three roles, and each role has a separate task. To summarize the process, the Requester submits a request, the Request Manager assesses and approves the request, and the Request Implementer carries out the request. But is it really that simple? Although it is very possible that a single role may submit a request, is it only the Request Manager that is involved in assessing and approving the request? If the request is complex, the Request Manager may involve additional people in assessing the request and possibly a team of people who discuss and then approve the request. So why should the process diagram have a swim lane that makes it appear as if only the Request Manager is carrying out that task? Similarly, in the Implement Request task, if the request is complex, it could involve a

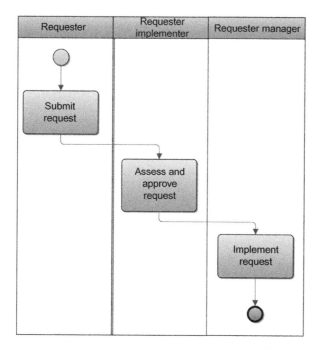

*Figure 5.2 Workflow with swim lanes.*

number of roles who carry out the task. In actuality, the swim lane typically only shows the role that is responsible for the task.

## 5.4 HORIZONTAL VERSUS VERTICAL WORKFLOWS

Workflows can be drawn either horizontally or vertically. This can seem like an insignificant issue, but it affects how your stakeholders understand your processes.

Most process modelers default to a horizontal, left-to-right workflow. That works well for fairly simple diagrams. See the simple horizontal workflow in Figure 5.3. It fits well onto the page.

What if the workflow was longer, as in Figure 5.4? Although the text and symbols are the same size in the tool I used to create this diagram, they shrank when I inserted the diagram onto this page. The smaller the text, the harder it is to read the workflow, and the harder it is for your stakeholders to understand the process you've modeled.

If this practice is left unchecked, it can lead to ludicrous results. I have seen some tiny workflows inserted into documents that were completely unreadable, such as the one in Figure 5.5.

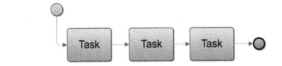

*Figure 5.3 Simple horizontal workflow.*

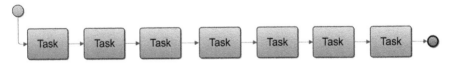

*Figure 5.4 Longer horizontal workflow.*

*Figure 5.5 Even longer horizontal workflow.*

One way to get around this is to wrap the workflow similar to the way text is wrapped in worksheets. The advantage of this is that the text can be made large enough to read. The disadvantage of workflow wrapping is that it can make swim lanes fatter as in Figure 5.6.

Another approach is to use continuation symbols to break up a lengthy workflow into two or more linked workflows. Figure 5.7 is one example. The first part of the workflow ends in link A. The second part of the workflow starts with link A. Those two workflows can then be described in different slides or in different parts of a document.

This brings us to another unfortunate fact. We typically have to communicate our workflows in either documents or slide decks. Documents are typically vertically (i.e., portrait) oriented, in an 8.5 × 11 format. Slide decks, on the other hand, are horizontally (i.e., landscape) oriented. If we create workflows for one medium, they may not work well in the other medium. If you pick one medium, it's best to stick with that medium to communicate your workflow. However, most of the time, we have to record our workflows in documents, which are vertical. For this reason, I favor creating vertical workflows.

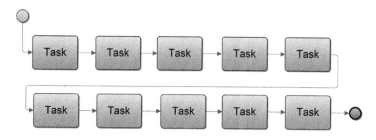

*Figure 5.6 Wraparound horizontal workflow.*

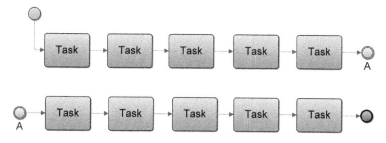

*Figure 5.7 Horizontal workflow separated into two parts.*

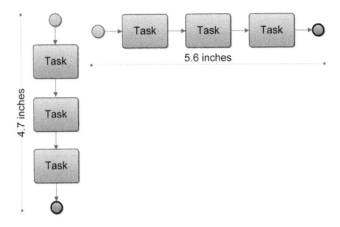

*Figure 5.8 Vertical workflows save space.*

Some people are very opposed to vertical workflows, believing they simply aren't acceptable. They somehow can't see that it's really the same workflows, albeit turned 90°. The advantage of vertical workflows is that they inherently provide you with more space to work with on within a document. If you happen to use swim lanes as well, it's simply a matter of rotating your swim lanes as well. (Note that some process modeling tools only allow you to create your workflows in either a vertical or horizontal direction. However, drawing tools typically provided allow you to do either.)

Vertical workflows can also have issues similar to horizontal workflows if they are too long, which means you might have to use wrap-around or linked workflows. However, you tend to run out of space less frequently with vertical workflows. This is because the text within task boxes always runs left-to-right, which means your text boxes will typically take up less space vertically than they do horizontally. In Figure 5.8, the vertical workflow takes up less actual space than the horizontal workflow.

My recommendation is to use vertical workflows.

## 5.5 GROUPING PROCESSES

If you have a large group of processes in your collection of processes, it is best to group them to more easily manage them. For instance, in ITIL(R), there are many processes organized into five groups.

Grouping processes allows you to refer to subsets of processes rather than having to name those processes individually. Of course, that's what grouping does in any context.

Putting the processes into groups is not easy. There may be a number of reasons behind why you will group your processes, such as

- Organization: Groupings that align most closely with organizational boundaries
- Functional similarity: Groupings that maximize functional affinity
- Systems: Groupings that most closely align with system scope
- Legacy: Groupings that align with terminology that is already known within the organization

Not all of the reasons are necessarily good reasons, but they may be reasons you have to live with.

## 5.6 ELEMENTAL PROCESSES

When possible, you should create your processes so that no process overlaps or duplicates the work done by another process. Such processes are called "elemental processes." In other words, they are the smallest set of individual processes that can be combined with other individual processes to do anything within the scope of your work.

This may seem obvious, but it's not always possible to create elemental processes. Often, an enterprise has separate organizations that created their own processes without regard to the processes that were created by other organizations within the enterprise. These processes may conflict with or duplicate other processes already in existence. When this happens, you may have to accept the existence of these other processes, even if they followed a very different approach.

## 5.7 SCENARIOS

The term "scenario" is used in many different contexts, so when you talk to other people about a scenario, you need to be specific and describe what that means. From a process perspective, a scenario is a description of a realistic business event that touches upon known processes. A scenario is a trip through parts of one or more processes in a way that is meaningful to the stakeholders of the modeling effort and

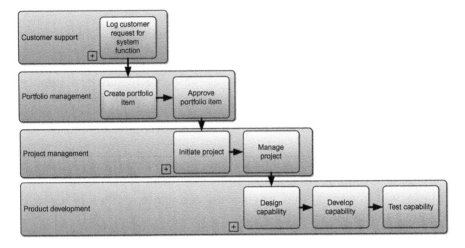

*Figure 5.9 Scenario diagram.*

useful for those that will implement the process. The most useful and interesting scenarios map to activities/tasks of multiple processes.

An example of a scenario is the following, which consists of a series of scenario steps and the corresponding Figure 5.9.

Scenario steps:

1. A customer contacts the customer help desk to request a new feature for a software product.
2. The new feature request is submitted as a new portfolio item to be considered.
3. The new request is approved for development.
4. A new development project is initiated.
5. The development project is managed and tracked.
6. The new feature is designed.
7. The new feature is developed.
8. The new feature is tested and released.

Obviously, additional detail and description could be provided for each step. Note how the steps of the scenario move through different activities within the various processes involved.

## 5.8 WORKFLOW PATTERNS

As you create more and more processes, you will begin to see similarities in the process workflows. In other words, some workflows will have similar types of work to be carried out. The context may be different, but the workflow is basically the same. These similar workflow segments are called "patterns." One very obvious workflow pattern involves filling out a form, checking it for obvious errors, and submitting it. There are many contexts in which this pattern may appear, such as submitting a help desk ticket, ordering an item, or submitting a change request.

Other obvious patterns include the following:

- Receiving a form, categorizing it, and initiating action on the form
- Reviewing and approving a request
- Analyzing options
- Reporting status
- Handling continuous improvement
- Evaluating a process and improving it

Identifying patterns typically does not happen during the initial definition of processes. It often happens after second, third, or subsequent passes through a process that patterns are noticed.

When patterns are identified, you should attempt to create a single generic workflow for that pattern and then apply that workflow wherever the pattern occurs in your processes. For instance, I earlier mentioned that there is a pattern for "evaluating a process and improving it." This occurs in practically every process. It typically involves collecting feedback and data, identifying new practices in industry, analyzing what did and did not work well, and deciding on what to change about the process. You can create activities and tasks that carry out that work in a generic workflow, then customize that pattern and apply it to each process.

# CHAPTER 6

## How to Fix a Bad Workflow

Sometimes, we are given a bad workflow and have to work with it. There's no need to spend your time criticizing the bad workflow. There are probably people who feel it is a real accomplishment. You should thank them for the workflow and ask them if you could make some minor adjustments to make it just a little better. In Chapter 1, I showed you a bad workflow that I was given. That workflow is shown again here. In the following sections, I will show you how you can fix that bad workflow.

It is not important that you make these fixes in the order shown in these sections. Your own situation may dictate that you do take steps in a different order, or that some steps may not be needed at all.

### 6.1 UNCOIL SNAKY WORKFLOWS

Workflows should go in a single direction: either top to bottom or left to right, depending on whether you are drawing vertical or horizontal workflows, respectively. This is because time is an important dimension in workflows. If your workflow goes backward, then the workflow is going backward in time. All workflows in a project and organization should follow a consistent approach. This helps adoption, implementation, and reduced time to value.

Some process modelers, probably trying to save space, will draw their workflows forward and backward, as shown in Figure 6.1. In this workflow, it is difficult at first glance to understand where the workflow ends. It takes a few moments to find how the workflow ends, and then you have to back up a bit visually to determine how you get there. Contrast this with a redrawn workflow, shown in Figure 6.2. This new figure uncoils the snaky workflow.

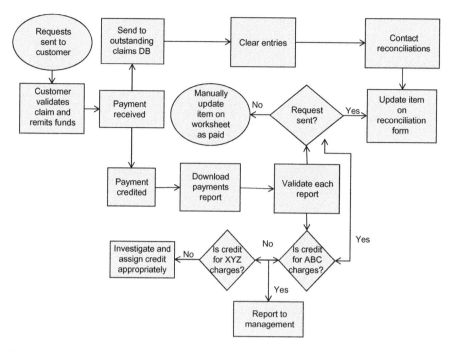

*Figure 6.1 Bad example revisited.*

In the redrawn workflow, the workflow is clearly top to bottom. It is easy to see the different threads of work and where they end.

Of course, there are still other things wrong with the workflow, but this is just the first step.

At this point, it may be useful to stop and show this redrawn workflow to the individuals who gave you the original workflow. Point out that it has the same information, just laid out differently. Most of the time, those individuals will immediately see the improvements.

## 6.2 UNRAVEL CONFUSING LOGIC

Even though the workflow is a little clearer, there are still a number of places in the workflow where it is unclear what the sequence of tasks is supposed to be. For instance, in Figure 6.2:

- Is Payment Received supposed to be a decision, or is it the start of parallel threads of work?
- The same for Validate Each Report

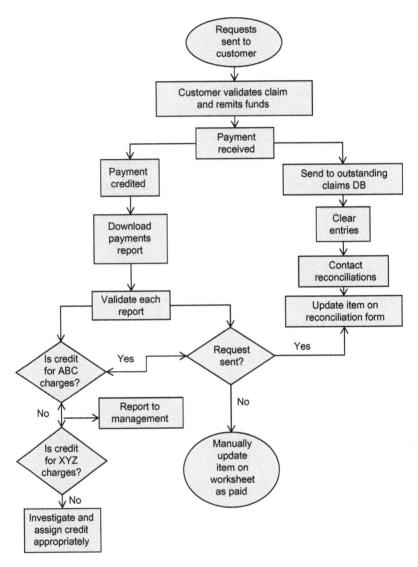

*Figure 6.2 Uncoiling the snaky workflow.*

- In the three decisions, where, exactly, do you go during a yes or no decision? What do the double-sided arrows mean?

You will have to ask the subject matter experts to clarify bad or unclear logic. In our example, we determine that both Payment Received and Validate Each Report are actually supposed to be

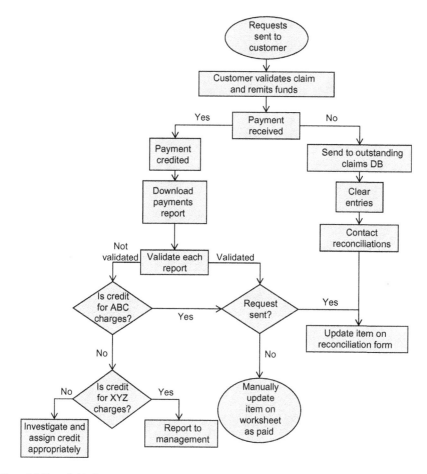

*Figure 6.3 Unraveled logic.*

decisions and that the double arrows are actually supposed to be single arrows. The resulting updated workflow is shown in Figure 6.3.

## 6.3 USE CONSISTENT NOTATION

Many inexperienced process modelers will be inconsistent in their notation. They aren't used to the subtleties that notation can convey. In our workflow, the most obvious inconsistency is the use of both circles and squares for the end of a workflow thread. Most workflow notations use some kind of circular symbol to indicate the end of a

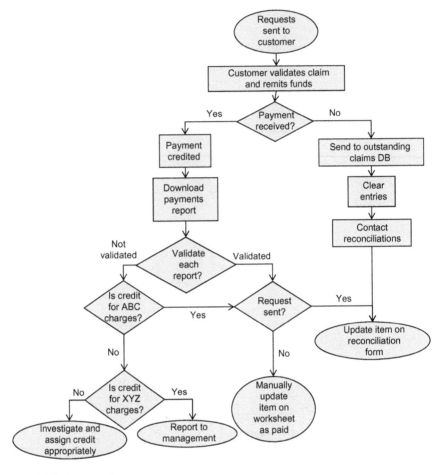

*Figure 6.4 Consistent notation.*

workflow thread, so we will use that convention as well. We also used diamond shapes for all decisions. The result is in Figure 6.4.

## 6.4 USE CONSISTENT NAMING

The final step in fixing a bad workflow is to change activity and task labels so they follow a standard pattern. This is described in more detail in "Naming Conventions." In our example, we will focus on

- Ambiguously named activities
- Uneven tasks
- Badly named activities

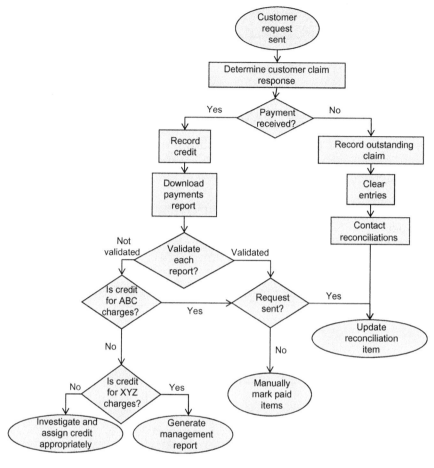

*Figure 6.5 Consistent naming.*

The resulting adjusted workflow is shown in Figure 6.5.

# CHAPTER 7

# Naming Conventions

## 7.1 USE A CONSISTENT NAMING STYLE

Consider the brief process workflow shown in Figure 7.1. This process involves creating and submitting a change order. It consists of three activities:

1. Form creation, initiation, and completion by user for system change order
2. Validation
3. Submit change order

These are all performed by the User role (Figure 7.1).

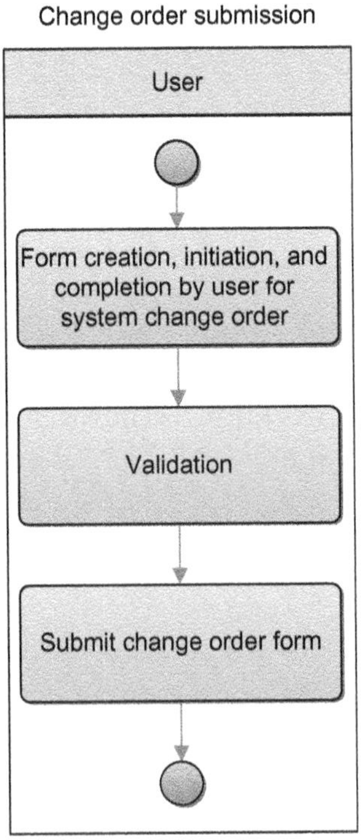

Change order submission

*Figure 7.1 Inconsistent naming style.*

The names of these three activities are very different in a couple of different ways. First, consider the length of the activity names. It's a bit like the story of the Three Bears. One is too long, one is too short, and one is "just right." The first activity (Form creation, initiation, and completion by user for system change order) is simply too long. Sometimes, a modeler tries to put too much information into an activity name, as if the modeler ignores the fact that the name is not the same as a description. The description of the activity can be elsewhere in the process documentation, but not in the diagram.

The second activity is simply named Validation. This is definitely shorter, but too short. Validation of what? How would this validation be different from the validation of something else in another process? A bit more contextual information should be added.

The third activity, "Submit Change Order" form, is the right length.

Another way these activity names are different, besides length, is the structure of the name. The first activity is a noun phrase. The second activity is a single verb. The third activity is a verb–noun phrase. All process items of the same type should follow the same style. As will be indicated in a subsequent section, I advocate that activities should be in the style of a verb–noun phrase.

Figure 7.2 shows a naming approach that is consistent.

## 7.2 ALL NAMES SHOULD BE UNIQUE

Although identifiers should be used, it is best to make sure all names are unique. This includes processes, activities, tasks, work products, and roles. Of course, distinct identifiers help distinguish one item from another. However, distinct names also help. Use contextual information to distinguish names. For example, if both the Change Management and Order Management processes contain an activity named "Review Request," you could change the two activities to be "Review Change Request" and "Review Order Request" so they identify their different contexts.

## 7.3 USE VERBS AND NOUNS IN A CONSISTENT WAY

As you begin to assign names to the items in your process models, you should attempt to use verbs and nouns in a consistent way. The names

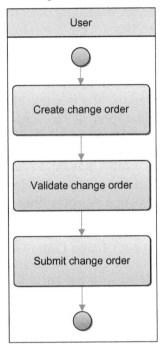

Change order submission

Figure 7.2 Consistent naming style.

of these items (i.e., processes, activities, tasks, roles, and work products) are fairly short, and readers obtain a tremendous amount of meaning from those few words in each name. It is important to use words consistently in order to convey meaning in a consistent way. For instance, consider the case where you have two activities named "Manage Payroll System" and "Administer Payment System." The words "manage" and "administer" are fairly similar. A person who sees those two names may wonder if "manage" means the same thing as "administer" or not. By changing the second activity to "Manage Payment System," you are communicating that the process is fairly equivalent in intent to "Manage Payroll System."

Concerning verbs, it is possible to identify a set of standard verbs for your team to use. In order to keep the list from being too constraining, you could identify a set of acceptable synonyms for each verb, noting that those synonyms actually mean the same as the standard verb.

For instance, the verb "analyze" may be the standard verb, but other acceptable verbs could be "evaluate," "investigate," and "study."

Concerning nouns, it is useful to carefully identify all of the primary business nouns you will use in your workflows. By "business noun," I do not mean specifically work products, although a business noun could represent a work product. For instance, if your process refers to change requests, portfolio items, or sales agreement, use those specific terms rather than "requests," "items," or "agreements," respectively.

## 7.4 NAMING PROCESSES

Processes should be named as an adjective–noun phrase. This is best practice within the industry. When someone talks about a process, they tend to want to discuss the process as a thing, not as an action. For example, it's more natural to say "How should we improve Incident Management?" than to say "How should we improve Manage Incidents?" Figure 7.3 shows a set of business processes for a small business called Feather Blimps. Notice that the term "Management" is used in most, but not all, process names.

Note that these are very high-level processes. These processes may themselves consist of other subprocesses.

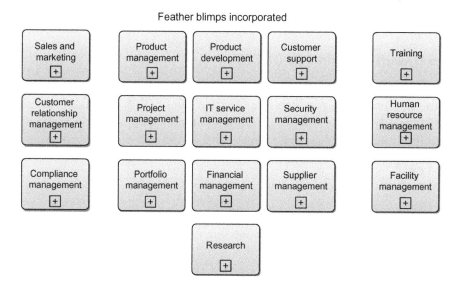

*Figure 7.3 Process naming example.*

An alternative would be to name processes as verb–noun phrases, similar to how activities and tasks are named. However, I tend to discourage this because this style makes process names too long. Examples of this approach include Communicate Management Aim and Direction, Assess and Manage Business Risks, and Manage Business Portfolio.

## 7.5 NAMING ACTIVITIES AND TASKS

Within a process, you typically want to know what work is done within the process. For that reason, activities and tasks are typically named with a verb–noun phrase. The verb indicates the action that is to be taken, and the noun indicates the thing on which the action is performed. See the diagram below, used earlier in this book. Each activity starts with a verb indicating what is going to be performed, such as "create," "validate," or "submit." Activities and tasks should be about 3–8 words in length. You should avoid lengthy activity and task names. This typically occurs when the process modeler attempts to summarize everything that takes place within an activity or task. This summary should instead be recorded in the activity/task description, not the name of the activity/task. Project managers and stakeholders may want to avoid creating anything other than diagrams, thinking the process is getting too detailed, but this kind of thinking should be discouraged. Descriptions are necessary for providing clarity to a process.

## 7.6 NAMING WORK PRODUCTS

Work products are typically assigned adjective–noun phrases. This is natural, since work products are tangible things. Work product names are typically 1–5 words long. Often, but not always, work products end in terms such as the following:

- Log
- List
- Plan
- Record
- Report
- Request
- Schedule
- Data

Examples of these include:

- Capacity Plan
- User Record
- Problem Report
- Change Request
- Development Schedule
- Asset Data

It is useful to use adjectives in work product names that indicate the primary process of the work product. This will help the reader understand the context of the work product and distinguish it from other work products that are similarly named. For instance, instead of having a work product merely named "Request" that is used within Change Management, it could be named "Change Request" to distinguish it from a "Supplier Request." Acronyms may be necessary in some instances where process names are lengthy.

## 7.7 NAMING ROLES

Role names are also important. Badly named roles can result in:

- Roles that represent either organizations or jobs and are therefore easily stretched or bent into things different than the intent of the modeler and defeat the goal of the modeling.
- Roles that are too large, and thus represent an unrealistically large scope of tasks for an individual skill set
- Roles that are too small, and make responsibility assignments unrealistically complex

Some of the rules of selecting role names include the following:

- Role names should help you identify the primary process in which they work. For instance, it is easy to remember that a Change Manager works within the Change Management process or that an Event Analyst works within the Event Management process. Of course, it is not always possible to create a role name that identifies the process in which the role works, but most of the time it is possible.

Role names should have a consistency to them. Consistency is important so you can distribute responsibilities in an equitable way. One way to promote consistency in role names is to use similarities in naming where possible. This works for many processes. For instance, many role names end in the following terms:

- Manager (e.g., Change Manager, Sales Manager, Portfolio Manager)
- Analyst (e.g., Market Analyst, System Analyst, Transaction Analyst)
- Administrator or Operator (e.g., System Administrator, Supply Administrator)
- Specialist (e.g., Version Control Specialist, Deployment Specialist, Communication Specialist)
- Representative (e.g., Service Representative, Vendor Representative)

You may have other common names to add to this list. Similarity in naming can help you

- Create predictable roles for processes
- Create predictable task responsibilities
- Write role descriptions using some commonality of language

In essence, role consistency will save your time in process modeling.

# CHAPTER 8

# Identifier Conventions

## 8.1 WHAT IS AN IDENTIFIER (ID)?

An identifier is a short code that is used to refer to a process or an element within a process. The code may be numeric only or a combination of alphabetic characters and numbers. It is best to indicate some kind of sequence to identifiers within a process group.

It is easiest to simply provide some examples of identifiers. For example, a Change Management process could be assigned an identifier such as CHG. The first activity within CHG could be referred to as CHG1. The first task within activity CHG1 could be referred to as CHG1.1.

## 8.2 WHY IDENTIFIERS ARE IMPORTANT

Identifiers are useful for referencing items in an abbreviated form. For instance, a process named "Change Order Submission" could be referred to as COS instead of the longer three-word name. This is useful in regular text, but is also very useful in diagrams, when there is not as much space for referencing items.

Consider the following diagram in Figure 8.1 for the COS process. The identifiers for the three activities in this process are COS1, COS2, and COS3. It's simpler to write "COS2" than "Validate change order."

Identifiers also carry contextual information as well. Notice that the COS3 activity flows into the COF1 activity, which is the first activity within the Change Order Fulfillment (COF) process. This very simple technique lets the reader know that the context is the first activity of the COF process.

Imagine how much more awkward it would be if you had to write out the entire context, as indicated in Figure 8.2.

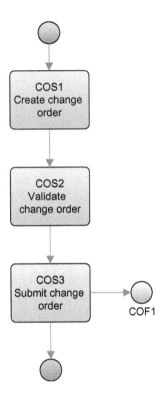

*Figure 8.1 Identifier example.*

Processes should be assigned a 3–4 letter identifier. It is best if you select a string of letters that easily help the reader associate the identifier with the item. For instance, "INC" could easily be associated with Incident Management.

Avoid identifiers that could be mistaken for more than one item. For instance, if you have both a Change Management process and a Channel Management process, do not use the identifier "CHM." Instead, use unambiguous identifiers. For instance, you could use CHG for Change Management and CNL for Channel Management.

Activities should be sequentially numbered, with the number added as a suffix to the process identifier, such as CHG1, CHG2.

Tasks within an activity should be numbered as well, but the task number should be separated from the activity number using a character such as a "." or "-". Examples include CHG1-1 or CHG1.1.

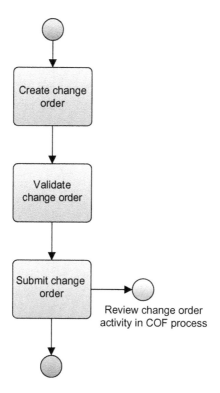

*Figure 8.2 Referencing a process without an ID.*

There is a problem with activity and task numbering. When activities or tasks are added or removed, it can wreak havoc on the nice organization of your process. For this reason, assign activity and task numbers late in process design. If you are reorganizing an existing process, it may be necessary to create matrices that indicate the activity and task numbering in the previous version of the process and the new version of the process.

## 8.3 WORK PRODUCT IDENTIFIERS

Identifiers should also be assigned to work products. Typically, a work product is created by a specific process. You should use the three-letter code for the process and add a "W" on the end (for "work product"). Append a number onto the end of that label. Examples include "CHGW-5" or "INCW-20."

## 8.4 ROLE IDENTIFIERS

In general, role identifiers are not needed. This may seem nonintuitive, since we have promoted using identifiers with processes, activities, tasks, and work products. However, there tend to be fewer roles, and role names typically do not take up much space in workflow diagrams.

# CHAPTER 9

# Workflow Connections and Relationships

## 9.1 WORKFLOW CONNECTIONS

Because process workflows consist of a sequence of activities or tasks, there are directional links to connect the items in a workflow. These connections are lines with unidirectional arrows, as shown in Figure 9.1.

Note that bidirectional connections would not work. This would completely ignore the sequential nature of a workflow. This may seem obvious, but I have seen many examples where bidirectional connections are used. Figure 9.2 is a type of workflow I have seen many times. In this example, the evaluation of a request is complex work. Evaluation (REQ2) includes categorization (REQ3) and analysis (REQ4) of the request before it can be handed off to make a decision on its approval. This is "probably" what is meant by the workflow, but it is unclear. If you were to apply standard workflow interpretation, the workflow would actually be more like the following:

1. Evaluate the request (REQ2)
2. Categorize the request (REQ3)
3. Analyze the request (REQ4)
4. When REQ4 is done, perform REQ3 again. (Obviously this would be an endless loop, because you would have to perform REQ4 again.)
5. When REQ3 is done, perform REQ2 again. (Another endless loop.)

You should keep workflows simple and avoid bidirectional connections.

You should also avoid any workflow that suggests an endless loop. There must always be a decision diamond or an event that allows you to break out of a loop.

There are three kinds of connections that can exist within a workflow:

1. Connections to or from other processes
2. Connections within the same workflow
3. Connections to or from start and stop nodes

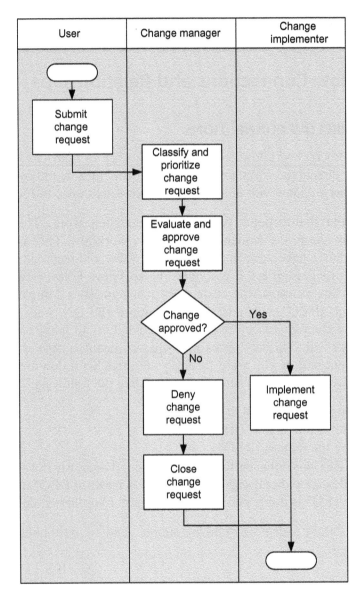

*Figure 9.1 Workflow connections.*

These are described in more detail in the following sections.

## 9.2 CONNECTIONS TO OR FROM OTHER WORKFLOWS

Workflows typically interface with other workflows. That is because workflows often use work products created by other workflows and

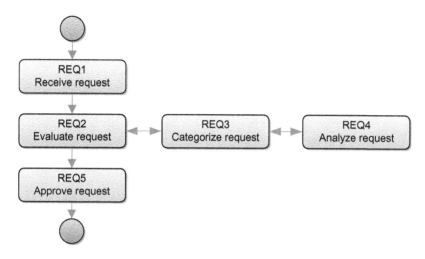

*Figure 9.2 Bidirectional arrows are unsuitable.*

vice versa. Connections to activities on a different page should be clearly marked by uniquely formatted "off page connectors." In Figure 9.3, there are several links to and from other processes. Note that the links have a different color to indicate they are from outside the process and that the links also use the reference ID of the specific activity in the other processes. (It should be noted that many process modeling notations and tools do not support this, but if you are using a drawing tool such as Visio, it's easy to do.)

## 9.3 CONNECTIONS WITHIN THE SAME WORKFLOW

Generally, connections within the same workflow are merely a matter of drawing an arrow from one activity/task to another activity/task. However, there are two issues that can come up. One issue is when an activity/task must connect to another activity/task in the workflow and there are too many other connections in the way to create an elegant-looking workflow. When that happens, there are two options, as shown in the complex workflow in Figure 9.4:

• The first option is to use a connection that appears to "cross over" another connection. See the connection from ABC11 to ABC3 as an example. This approach typically works well unless the diagram starts to become too busy visually. When this happens, it is best to use the second option.

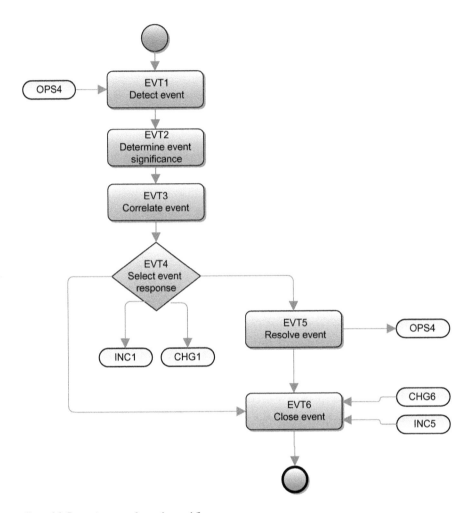

*Figure 9.3 Connections to or from other workflows.*

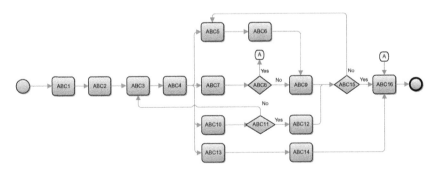

*Figure 9.4 Connections within a workflow.*

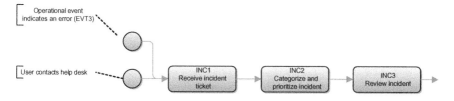

*Figure 9.5 Start node annotation.*

- The second option is to use link symbols. Note that one of the connections from decision ABC8 goes to ABC16. In this example, a link symbol (the yellow A) is used to link those two items. If you drew the connection completely between ABC8 to ABC16, it would have to cross over two other connections. It's subjective whether you feel that is too busy visually or not.

## 9.4 CONNECTIONS TO OR FROM START AND STOP NODES

Start and stop nodes typically, but not always, represent interfaces with other workflows or processes. Start nodes indicate how a process starts. Modern notations such as Business Process Modeling Notation (BPMN) typically make use of things like events to indicate how a process starts. Nevertheless, you should indicate what starts a workflow. In Figure 9.5, there are two start nodes for the workflow. One of them is an incident passed to this process from another process (Event Management). The other start node is not from a specific process, but just something that occurs outside the process. (The entire workflow is not shown.)

Similarly, stop nodes should indicate the destination of work or work products from the workflow.

## 9.5 PROCESS RELATIONSHIPS

Processes are typically related to other processes. That is because the work that is done by one process often affects other processes. For instance, a process that orders supplies is affected by the process that receives those supplies. Or a process that receives requests from a customer is affected by the process that fulfills those requests.

However, it is important to identify two specifically different types of relationships between processes. Figure 9.6 illustrates one kind of process diagram I have seen many times. In this diagram, the output of the process Receive Item Order is an input into the process Ship Item.

*Figure 9.6 Processes with indirect relationships.*

At a very high level, there is an upstream/downstream relationship between these two processes. In other words, the result of the first process brings about the second process. Although this is true, in most businesses, it is rare that a work product created by the first process is actually an input work product into the second process.

A more realistic process diagram would be that shown in Figure 9.7. There are additional processes between Receive Item Order and Ship Item, such as those to process the payment and another one to receive the item from the warehouse. Note also the work products output from each process that feed into the next process.

Unfortunately, some process modelers fail to distinguish between those processes that have direct relationships and those that have indirect relationships. In a direct relationship, the output of one process is the input of another relationship and is transformed to create one or more work products. Figure 9.7 is an example of processes with direct relationships.

In contrast, Figure 9.6 is an example of processes with indirect relationships. Processes with indirect relationships do not feed specific work products from one process to the next. Instead, the general results, both tangible and intangible, of one process have an effect on another process. Process models with indirect relationships may be useful for very high-level discussions, strategy documents, or "marketectures," but they are not accurate process models.

## 9.6 WORK PRODUCTS

As indicated earlier, a work product is a "tangible result of work." A work product may exist in either a soft copy or hard copy form.

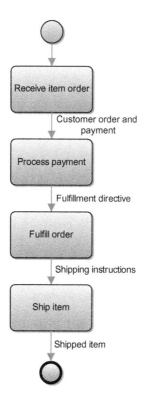

*Figure 9.7 Processes with direct relationships.*

It may be an electronic file or may exist in printed form. It should be remembered that it is objective, tangible, discoverable, and auditable. An objective third party should be able to discover and identify the work product.

A work product should not be an intangible result of work, such as "trained employees," "satisfied customer" or being "aligned with business objectives." These may be outcomes of the work, but they are not work products. Instead of trained employees, you may want to have a work product that indicates employees are trained, such as an employee training report. Instead of a satisfied customer as a work product, you might want to have a customer satisfaction report.

As indicated below, there are different kinds of work products.

## 9.7 ARTIFACTS

An artifact is an intermediate work product that is created in support of a customer deliverable. For example, System Test Results may be created prior to the creation of a System Test Report. The System Test Results artifact describes what happened during testing, whereas the System Test Report contains the results organized, described, and summarized for the test stakeholders.

Artifacts tend to be less formal than deliverables, since the latter are actually provided to stakeholders.

## 9.8 DELIVERABLES

A deliverable is a formal work product that is provided to stakeholders. The data and information is structured in such a way that it provides sufficient clarity and usability to the stakeholder. This is true whether the deliverable is a report or a collection of data. The report is understandable to the stakeholder who reads it, and the collection of data can be used by a stakeholder's system.

Managers are typically interested in tracking deliverables, but are less interested in tracking artifacts.

## 9.9 INPUTS, OUTPUTS, AND CONTROLS

A work product exists as an input, an output, or a control. An input provides data or information needed to perform an activity or task. That data or information is then transformed into an output. For instance, a Change Request that is input into an activity may result in a Change Order that is output from that same activity.

Often, there are multiple inputs and multiple outputs. Each input may come from different activities/tasks, and each output may go to different activities/tasks.

It is important to remember the distinction between inputs and outputs. Inputs are somehow transformed by an activity/task to create an output.

A work product may sometimes be both an input and an output of an activity/task. This happens if the work product increases in complexity or detail as it is passed from task to task, such as a data record or form. For instance, a Change Request may be input to a Categorize Request activity. That activity assigns and enters the category data

*Figure 9.8 Adding the state to the work product name is a bad idea.*

into the Change Request, then outputs the same Change Request with that additional information. When a work product is both an input and an output, process modelers are often tempted to put some kind of state information into the work product name, for instance, see Figure 9.8. The input is "Change Request" and the output is "Change Request (categorized)." This approach should be avoided because someone will treat these as two different work products when it is really the same work product. Putting state information into the work product name may seem like useful information, but it often results in the creation of unnecessary or duplicate work products. Having a limited number of standardized work products enables better work product management.

A "control" is a work product that contains reference information that is needed by the activity/task to produce the output. Examples include:

- Business rules: Typically used to constrain or channel how work is done
- Customer information: Provides information to sales, marketing, support, or other roles that help provide specific messages to a customer
- Standard operating procedures: Help guide the work being done in a task, such as troubleshooting

There is a tendency to combine inputs and controls in a modeling effort. This needlessly expands the list of inputs. By separating inputs from controls, you are able to simplify the list of inputs, increasing the understandability of your process.

## 9.10 CONTAINER WORK PRODUCTS

Container work products hold or encompass other work products. For instance, within an activity, there might be multiple artifact work products that contain information that are to be bundled into a larger deliverable work product. An example might be an Incident Log and an Incident Trend Analysis that are bundled into a larger Support Effectiveness Report. Containers are primarily useful for aggregating information in existing work products into a new comprehensive work product.

# CHAPTER 10

# Roles

Roles are the entities that perform the actions carried out by a process. Roles can represent individuals, teams, or systems that carry out work, participate with other roles, or are accountable for the work. Each role represents a work function to be performed, a collection of duties to be done, divorced from job titles and organizational boundaries.

Examples of roles include "Customer Support Analyst," "Disaster Planner," and "Salesperson."

## 10.1 WHAT ROLES ARE

Roles are what people do. Roles describe a responsibility a person or system has. Roles are combined into jobs. While in a large organization a single role may be a single job, in a small organization it would be very rare that a single role would be a single job. Because responsibilities persist, roles do as well. For instance, a salesperson is a role because it is a responsibility a person has. Within an organization, someone who sells products or services is a salesperson, regardless of whether they actually are called that or not.

Roles may represent a team if that team acts as a single entity. For instance, if a team collectively makes a single decision, you could represent that team as a single role. (Of course, if you wanted to model the decision-making process itself, you would probably have to split up the team into separate roles to model how the various individuals contribute to the final decision.)

## 10.2 WHAT ROLES ARE NOT

Roles are not job titles. Job titles change over time and from organization to organization. For instance, a salesperson may have the title of "Customer Representative," "Associate," or "Customer Specialist," depending on the organization. However, if their responsibility is to sell to customers, each of them has the role of a salesperson.

Although roles can represent teams when they work as a single unit, a role rarely, if ever, represents an organization. Typically, an organization includes individuals who have many different responsibilities. Instead, an organization should be represented by a number of roles for each of those responsibilities.

Care should be taken, however, not to make responsibilities too fine-grained. If responsibilities are too small, your process models become unnecessarily complex. Basically, if responsibilities are typically combined into a single individual, then you should not divide them.

## 10.3 ROLE RELATIONSHIPS WITH WORK PRODUCTS

Roles are the agents that create, modify, and use work products. Because of this, roles have a relationship with work products.

Some roles *own* work products. A role who owns a work product has responsibility for the content of that work product. They may or may not actually create the content, but they ensure that the content is created.

Other roles create the content of a work product. These are workers who take information and knowledge from other sources and transform it into content for another work product. Roles may be solely responsible for the content of a work product or may participate with other roles to create a work product. These roles are *creators* of work products.

Roles also use work products as reference materials. These may be policies, rules, decision tables, procedures, studies, background materials, etc. Roles who use work products in this way are *readers* of work products.

## 10.4 ROLE INVOLVEMENT WITH PROCESSES

Just as roles have responsibilities related to work products, they also have responsibilities associated with workflows. Typically, these are communicated through RACI charts.

RACI charts identify how roles participate in each task of a workflow. That participation may fall into one of the following four categories:

1. Responsible: Carries out the task
2. Accountable: Final accountability for the task (note that there should only be one role who has accountability)
3. Consulted: Provides opinion or feedback on a task
4. Informed: Made aware of the results of the task

A RACI chart is a matrix that maps roles against the tasks in a workflow. Each cell in the matrix is marked with an R, A, C, or I, based on the role's participation. Some teams who create RACI charts become confused about how to assign RACI participation. For example:

- Responsibility and Accountability are often difficult to differentiate, primarily because roles are not always clear about what they are accountable for or sometimes even what accountability means.
  - Accountability is allocated to ensure a single entity is answerable for cost, quality, performance, outcomes and risk related to actions, decisions, and performance. The accountability may be based on regulation or agreement or through delegated assignment.
  - Responsibility is an assigned requirement or obligation to act and take decisions to achieve required outcomes.
  - A role may be reluctant to identify themselves as being accountable. This is good because accountability is an important designation. Instead, accountability should be designated from above.
  - When a role is both responsible and accountable, it is designated as either "R/A" or "R, A."
- There can also be confusion about the distinction of "consulted" versus "informed." That is because communication patterns between roles are not always well understood.
  - "Consulted" indicates a requirement for a two-way conversation. This means that the Consulted role is informed; the Consulted role has a responsibility to analyze the information and respond with the results of their analysis. Information is required to be provided, and a response back is also required.
  - When a role is merely "Informed," it indicates that information must be provided but there is no requirement to provide feedback or for anyone to listen to the feedback if it is provided.
  - When a role should be both consulted and informed, it is designated as either "C/I," or "C, I."

# CHAPTER 11

# Useful Process Documents

The following are useful documents to create in the course of designing processes.

## 11.1 PROCESS CATALOG

A process catalog is a list of processes that are organized in some logical manner such as alphabetically, by category, or by similarity. This catalog focuses on the process workflows, decomposing into activities and tasks. It also identifies the roles and work products that are involved in the workflows.

## 11.2 ROLE CATALOG

A role catalog is a list of roles involved in the process workflows. This catalog contains a description of each role and identifies how each role is related to the workflows and work products. The catalog may also contain some categorization of the work products. Because most roles do their work completely or mostly within the context of a single process the modeler may categorize roles by process.

## 11.3 WORK PRODUCT CATALOG

A work product catalog is a list of work products involved in the process workflows. Each work product has an associated description. Because work products typically originate in specific processes, it may be pertinent to categorize work products by the processes in which they originated. It may be necessary to merely list the work products alphabetically if associating them with specific processes only works for a subset of the work products.

## 11.4 PROCESS INTERFACE MATRIX

Processes interface with other processes. That is, the work products of processes are sent or transferred to other processes. To capture those interfaces, you should create a process interface matrix. This matrix is a table that lists the processes in the row and column headers. The matrix is useful for process owners to understand which other processes are their stakeholders and should participate in process-related governance boards. The entries in the matrix indicate which processes interface with other processes. If you are ambitious, you can indicate within the matrix which work product is passed from one process to another, but that is dependent on the size and complexity of the matrix. A simple example of this matrix is shown below.

| | Asset Management | Customer Service | Development | Financial Management | Order Management | Portfolio Management | Research | Supplier Management | Sales and Marketing |
|---|---|---|---|---|---|---|---|---|---|
| Asset Management | n/a | | | x | x | | | x | |
| Customer Service | | n/a | | | x | | x | | x |
| Development | | | n/a | | | x | x | | x |
| Financial Management | x | | | n/a | x | x | | x | |
| Order Management | x | x | | x | n/a | | | x | |
| Portfolio Management | | | x | x | | n/a | x | | |
| Research | | | x | | | x | n/a | | |
| Supplier Management | x | | | x | x | | | n/a | |
| Sales and Marketing | | x | | x | | | | | n/a |

## 11.5 WORK PRODUCT PARTICIPATION MATRIX

The Work Product Participation Matrix is a table that shows how work products are related to processes. A work product can be shown as an input (I), output (O), or reference (R) (sometimes called a "control") to a process. Because there tend to be a large number of work products, it is often best to have a separate table for each process. An example of this matrix is shown below.

| | Asset Management | Customer Service | Development | Financial Management | Order Management | Portfolio Management | Research | Supplier Management | Sales and Marketing |
|---|---|---|---|---|---|---|---|---|---|
| Asset List | O | | | | | | | | |
| Asset Deployment Order | O | | | | | | | | |
| Service Request | | O | | | | | | | |
| Customer Communication | | O | | | | | | | |
| Requirements | | | O | | | | | | |
| Test Plan | | | O | | | | | | |
| Project Plan | | | O | | | | | | |
| Purchase Requisition | | | | | I | | | | |
| Purchase Order | | | | | O | | | | |
| Account Information | | | | O | | | | | |
| Expense Record | | | | I | | | | | |
| Portfolio Item | | | | | | O | | | |
| Business Strategy | | | | | | I | | | |
| Research Proposal | | | | | | | O | | |
| Research Results | | | | | | | O | | |
| Ordered Items | | | | | | | | O | |
| Vendor Evaluation | | | | | | | | O | |
| Sales Forecast | | | | | | | | | O |
| Product Information | | | O | | | | | | I |
| Sales Results | | | | | | | | | O |

# CHAPTER 12

# Tools

There are a variety of process-related tools. The primary types of tools are those involved in modeling. Although we have focused on modeling tools, this chapter will discuss other process-related tools.

## 12.1 DRAWING TOOLS

The most basic type of tool used to create processes is a drawing tool. Drawing tools are very flexible, which allows users to use any type of graphic elements to construct the process. However, this is also a drawback, because it can be difficult to enforce standards using just a drawing tool. Many modeling tools can import diagrams created by drawing tools. The most frequent drawing tool used is Microsoft Visio. In many organizations, Visio is the only process-related tool.

## 12.2 MODELING TOOLS

Modeling tools are a step up from mere drawing tools. Modeling tools are used to create persistent process elements, such as tasks, roles, and work products that can be reused. This means that, if you create a role such as a user in one process, you can easily reuse that role in another process without having to redefine that role.

In addition, a process element contains additional information such as a description of the element, links to related elements, and usage and guidance information. Thus, when you reuse an element, you are reusing not only the depiction of that element, but also its description and any additional information about that element. With a drawing tool, you are, at best, only reusing the graphic depiction of that element.

Modeling tools also can enforce notation standards such as BPMN. This makes it much easier to make your process models look the same, although you will still need to review process models to make them similar.

It is recommended that you use a process modeling tool, not just a drawing tool. You will be able to accomplish much more than simple drawing tools. However, the cost may not be justifiable for your project.

## 12.3 SIMULATION TOOLS

Simulation tools allow you to run simulations of processes in order to optimize performance times and resource allocations. Simulation is important if there are questions about performance or if process improvement is a goal of your project. However, simulation is generally not needed in most process-related projects.

## 12.4 PUBLISHING TOOLS

Once a process has been designed, it must be published so it can be followed. The simplest approach to this is drawing your process in Visio and then copying the process parts to a presentation or other user accessible document. This may be all that is necessary in many projects, but many modeling tools have a different publishing capability. Publishing a process that contains a hierarchy of decompositions and interfaces with other processes is not a simple job. Many modeling tools inherently contain a publishing capability. The best publishing tools will publish to a separate web site, allowing process consumers to easily click through the various process decompositions and related roles and work products.

Publishing is also very useful during process design when process subject matter experts (SMEs) need to validate a process. The capability to enter comments about the process directly into the published site can help facilitate the review cycle.

It is recommended that you use modeling tools with both a web publishing capability and commenting capability.

## 12.5 REVIEWING TOOLS

When creating process models, you should have tools that allow your SMEs to review your processes and provide their feedback to you. Although they could provide this information simply in an e-mail or document, it is more effective if the publishing tool you are using also

allows reviewers to enter their comments directly into the diagrams you have created. The reviewing tools should not allow the reviewers to modify your diagrams but simply create annotations wherever they want inside your diagrams. This approach makes it much easier to identify specifically where changes are needed in the diagrams. Advanced reviewing tools allow you as modeler to reply to a comment and even provide some indication concerning whether the comment was implemented or not.

## 12.6 EXECUTION TOOLS

The end result of a process modeling project may simply be the model itself. However, many times the end result is an implemented set of processes. These processes may be implemented via a series of human procedures and system functions that are integrated in a sequence. However, processes may also be implemented using an execution engine. An execution engine can turn a process design into an actual working process. However, there is usually lots of additional detail that must be added to a design to make it executable. Using a process execution engine typically requires specialized implementation skills that are not usually found among process modelers, so be prepared to expend additional time finding individuals with the right skills to utilize your process execution engine. Process models can be developed directly in tools that configure tool automated workflows. In other cases, the process modeling tools may need to export data into a different format than can then be imported into the workflow automation engine. In other cases, workflow drawings may be used in high-level design work but configuring automated workflows may be a separate effort.

# CHAPTER *13*

## Conclusion: Which Style Elements Are Right for Your Team?

As you go through the style elements described in this book, you have probably identified those elements that you think will work for your team. Make a list of those elements. Then, you should consider how you want to introduce those elements to your team.

You are probably already aware that many process modelers are fairly independent-minded and may already have their own style. As such, it is not easy to get them to embrace new techniques. This is the same behavior exhibited by many software developers, both in the past and today. However, many development organizations have learned to accept some form of guidelines and standards. Those guidelines and standards help them work together as a team.

The ideas in this book are my style. They may not be your team's style. Your team may only embrace some (or none) of my style elements. You may have better style elements than I have. I hope this book will help you begin the creation of your team's style.

Here are some ideas that may help you introduce these ideas to your team:

- Start small: As mentioned, process modelers tend to be very independent-minded and feel their own style works just fine. Don't give them a lot of things to that they have to comply with at first. Start with a small number of elements. Give them plenty of examples. Let them have a period of time to try out those elements. If they do not have any big objections, then make them your best practices and enforce them in your process reviews.
- Abandon practices that don't work: Some style elements seem good at first but later prove to have little value. In a team I worked in, we adopted several style elements that no one had used before. Years later, we realized that we never needed to use them, so we dropped them. Many times, we have good ideas about what we should do, but they aren't "best practices." Best practices are just

that—things people have been using for quite some time that really work. Unfortunately, there are many good ideas that we parade around as "best practices." In other words, they were ideas someone thought had value but had never really used in practice. Those may be good when you are first forming your modeling team, but they won't last unless they truly are practices your team members find useful. Whenever you hear the term "best practice" you should immediately remove the word "best" and realize they are merely practices that someone at one time thought were best. They may have become leading practices, good practices, or "old practices" by the time you are executing your project.

- Incorporate new style elements from your team: Although I would be really flattered if you started out with only style elements you found from my book, you should search your team for style elements that have worked for them. Ask them for ideas. Ask them what helped them. Select a small number (remembering to keep it small at first) that seem to be the best ones and include them in your team's style.
- Revisit your team's style and improve: Document your team style and let it remain for awhile. Enforce the style in your reviews. At least once a year, give your team the opportunity to review and comment on your published team style. What worked? What didn't work? What else should we include? Let them own your team style and they will much more readily embrace it.

As mentioned earlier, this book represents my style. Undoubtedly, you will come up with ideas that will improve upon what I have described here. I hope you will share those ideas with me. My contact information is available on the author's page.

There are a number of standards related to processes that you should consider complying with. These are international standards created under the oversight of the International Organization for Standardization (ISO). Compliance with these standards may not be necessary with your project unless your processes need to integrate with those of other enterprises. However, these standards also provide important guidelines that may be useful to you even if you don't need to comply with ISO standards.

## A.1 ISO 9001

ISO 9001 is an international standard for quality management systems. As such, it describes the requirements for a quality management system that manages the quality of products or services. This standard has become very popular across a number of industries, and it has a lot to say about how processes are defined. According to ISO 9001, management processes should be:

- Documented: Described in a document
- Measurable: Quantified in a tangible way
- Integrated: Designed so they work together
- Implemented: In operation, not just designed
- Objectively assessable: Able to be evaluated for continuous improvement

An organization following ISO 9001 will:

- Identify the processes that make up the quality management system
- Define the inputs and outputs of each process
- Define the sequential workflow of the processes and how they interact
- Determine the consequences of unintentional process outcomes
- Define how to determine the effectiveness of the process
- Define roles and responsibilities
- Determine authority over each process

- Define the work needed to implement each process
- Define the approach for continuous improvement

ISO 9001 is popular for supply chain processes. Some businesses require ISO 9001 compliance for that reason.

## A.2 ISO 33000 AND ISO IEC 15504

ISO 33000 and ISO IEC 15504 establish international standards for describing processes and assessing process capabilities. Because process implementation typically includes improving process capabilities over time, these international standards provide "a standard approach" to improving process capability and organizational maturity.

According to these standards, each process should contain the following:

- Process name: A brief noun phrase that summarizes the process scope and is unique. The name should indicate the primary objective of the process.
- Process context: The ecosystem in which the process operates
- Process purpose: A high-level statement or statements of the overall goal of the process. The purpose clearly distinguishes the process from other processes but does not list everything performed by the process.
- Process outcomes: Observable results of the successful operation of the process. This does not include work products, but are measurable and tangible results. The outcomes consist of a list of such results.
- Base practices: The primary capabilities of this process
- Information work products: Inputs and outputs of the process, including high-level information requirements of each work product. Typically, work products should fall into one of the following categories:
  a. Description
  b. Plan
  c. Procedure
  d. Record
  e. Report
  f. Request
  g. Specification
- Interfaces: How the process interacts with other processes

These are described in more detail below. Refer to the standards themselves for definitive information.

### A.2.1 Process Context

The process context describes the environment in which the process operates. This is important, because it may be possible for the process to work within different contexts. For example, a change management process may work within engineering, development or acquisition context, or an operations context.

### A.2.2 Base Practices

Base practices are the primary activities within a process. Rather than provide a concise set of process workflows, base practices focus on the actions that are performed by a process. Base practices are the set of specific activities that are required to produce the process outcomes. They do not need to be sequential. They are the process activities for which an auditor should be able to find evidence. Base practices are useful, but unless workflows are defined as well, those who are supposed to practice/implement the process are left to create their own workflows, which could cause further confusion. Base practices would be the minimum set of activities that must be performed to produce the process outcomes rather than every practice that an expert thinks is "best."

### A.2.3 Interfaces

Process and organizational information interfaces should include the following:

- The information work products that are sent from one process to another, including designating the sending process and the receiving process
- Descriptions of the information exchanged between the business and its suppliers